The Makings
of Happiness

Also by Ronald Wallace

POETRY

Plums, Stones, Kisses & Hooks, 1981
Tunes for Bears to Dance To, 1983
People and Dog in the Sun, 1987

POETRY CHAPBOOKS

Installing the Bees, 1977
Cucumbers, 1977
The Facts of Life, 1979
The Owl in the Kitchen, 1985

CRITICISM

Henry James and the Comic Form, 1975
*The Last Laugh: Form and Affirmation in the
    Contemporary American Comic Novel*, 1979
*God Be With the Clown: Humor in American
    Poetry*, 1984

ANTHOLOGY

*Vital Signs: Contemporary American Poetry
    from the University Presses*, 1989

The Makings
of Happiness

RONALD WALLACE

University of Pittsburgh Press

The publication of this book is supported by grants from the National Endowment for the Arts in Washington, D.C., a Federal agency, and the Pennsylvania Council on the Arts.

Published by the University of Pittsburgh Press, Pittsburgh, Pa. 15260
Baker & Taylor International
Manufactured in the United States of America

Library of Congress Cataloging-in-Publication Data

Wallace, Ronald.
    The makings of happiness / Ronald Wallace.
      p.   cm. — (Pitt poetry series)
    ISBN 0-8229-3669-0 (cloth). — ISBN 0-8229-5448-6 (pb.)
    I. Title. II. Series.
    PS3573.A4314M35   1991
    811'.54—dc20   90-21292
                                                        CIP

The author and publisher wish to express their grateful acknowledgment to the following publications in which some of these poems first appeared: *The Atlantic* ("Breakdown," "Wiffle Ball"); *Blue Unicorn* ("Condoms"); *Crazyhorse* ("Fresh Oysters & Beer," "In the Amish Bakery"); *The Cream City Review* ("Building an Outhouse," "Hairpin"); *The Georgia Review* ("State Poetry Day"); *Kansas Quarterly* ("Professor of Plums"); *The Laurel Review* ("Early Brass," "The Fox in the Berry Patch," "Onions," "Speeding"); *Negative Capability* ("Turning Forty"); *Poetry* ("Apple Cider," "The Fat of the Land," "Love and Sex," "The Poetry Report," "Smoking"); *Poetry Miscellany* ("Fortunes"); *Poetry Northwest* ("Camp Calvary," "Fall," "Frogs," "The Makings of Happiness," "Off the Record," "Poet in the Goat Yard"). *Prairie Schooner* ("Bluegills," "Headlines," "The Hell Mural: Panel I," "The Hell Mural: Panel II"); *The Seattle Review* ("The Dinner Party"); *Shenandoah* ("Basketball"); *The Southern Review* ("Birdsong, Anyway," "Fan Mail," "Prayer"); *Sou'wester* ("Barn Swallows," "Burning"); *Tar River Poetry* ("Astronomy," "At Forty," "Rebounding," formerly "Basketball"); *Wisconsin Poets Calendar* ("February, Full Moon," "Roosters"); *Yankee* ("February Thaw") and *Yarrow: A Journal of Poetry* ("Night in the Country").

"Wiffle Ball" was reprinted in *The Fireside Book of Baseball* (Simon & Schuster, 1987). "Barn Swallows" and "Burning" were reprinted in *The Anthology of Magazine Verse* (Monitor Book Co., 1987). "Smoking" was reprinted in *Sweet Nothings: An Anthology of Rock and Roll in American Poetry* (Spoon River Poetry Press, 1990). "State Poetry Day" was reprinted in *The Anthology of Magazine Verse* (Monitor Book Co., 1991).

I wish to thank the Wisconsin Arts Board (in conjunction with the National Endowment for the Arts), the Wisconsin Alumni Research Foundation, the William F. Vilas Trust, and the Robert E. Gard Wisconsin Idea Foundation for their generous support.

Cover painting of "The Photographer" by Nick Engelbert from a photograph by Maurice Thaler, used by permission of Maurice Thaler and Kohler Foundation, Inc. Special thanks to Katie Kazan, Maurice Thaler, Lou Ann and Lincoln Engelbert, Lynne Eich, and Ruth DeYoung Kohler.

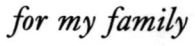

for my family

*"If a man can't be happy on a little farm in Wisconsin,
he hasn't the makings of happiness in his soul."*

—Nick Engelbert, artist-farmer, 1881–1962

Contents

III. The Makings of Happiness

I. Early Brass

Early Brass

When five balding men in long-tailed tuxedos
rise to the bright occasion, their brass
sacbuts, cornet, and slide trumpet in hand, O
the chansons and canzoni, the madrigals, the sass
they pull out of their bold embouchures! Their bravado's
a coinage of lieder and light so daft
no music could, under sweet heaven, surpass
the New York Cornet & Sacbut Ensemble's.

Yet last night in the lunchroom of Van Hise School,
when my sixth-grade daughter and her oversized trombone—
all silverware, sour milk, and John Philip Sousa—
sashayed on stage at a slapstick recital,
she sounded (by God!) not altogether un-
like the New York Cornet & Sacbut Ensemble.

Bluegills

Fast in the wire mesh basket
tied to the dock, six bluegills,
duped by dazzle and subterfuge,
shimmer and flick. My daughter,
reeling in my permission,
is about to let them out.
Oh, don't, her great-aunts shout,
that's money in the bank, that's dinner.
Out in the bay a great blue
heron rudders and swoops,
scooping up light and silver.

It's a stand-off: my poor daughter
poised on the dock; my aunts,
hackles up, in a fluster;
the rich fish slipping
from their narrow enclosure;
and me, who only wants everybody
happy, on this bright day
getting darker, eating my words
as if that could save
anyone, cast off
the world's great hunger.

Fresh Oysters & Beer

I'm lifting the oysters
up from the ice chips,
scooping the slippery pap
loose with a spoon,
dripping the sliver of lemon, the ripe
island of tabasco, and then
flipping it all up to my lip and sipping
it in, the rough texture of shell
on incisor, the limp liquidy tongue
poised for the pleasure
of soft palate and swallow, and
the following chilled schooner of beer.
Meanwhile, my rampantly
adolescent daughter, vegetarian and
teetotaler, is squirming, her frown
brown and decaying on her face.
She's eating her breadsticks
and lettuce, the tofu and lentils
she's smuggled in under her sweatshirt,
a bundle of grimace and disgust.
Can't we see, she screams, *that's
a creature!* as the patrons of happy
hour turn toward us, and the taste-
fully well-endowed waitresses
in their wet T-shirts emblazoned
"I got the crabs at Cap'n Kurt's"
stop to scratch their saucy behinds.
A creature! she shrieks, exasperated,
as Cap'n Kurt sticks his head
out of the sizzling kitchen, rolls
the oyster-like whites of his eyes
at the fat bouncer in the far corner,
who gets up slowly and comes toward us,

as I flip a bill from my wallet,
and we exit, meek as vegetables,
me and my steamy daughter
just so much meat in his eyes.

Birdsong, Anyway

I hung it behind the house,
this lumbering feeder so large
no self-respecting bird would utter
a kernel of song about it:

slung from the lowest branch
like a broken limb in traction,
the plexiglass scrawled with signatures
of niger seed, sunflower, suet.

In sixth grade I knew a girl so fat
no ordinary desk could hold her;
she sat on the playground after lunch
affixed to the chain link fence,

all my skinny friends aflutter,
kicking her rubbery shins as if
they cared at all about her.
Nancy Bowers, my secret sixth-grade lover,

your memory is so large, even
thirty long years later
I still can't see around it
as I watch pine siskins, juncoes, grossbeaks

banging on the feeder, knocking
my good intentions asunder,
pecking the plexiglass dry.
I'll sing about anything, now.

Rebounding

All thumbs, clown
of the key and back court, king
of the limp pass and spastic dribble,
I knew I was no
Alcindor. Still,
one season, I remember,
everything I threw up to the rim
went in:
the defense doing double takes
at the net's appreciative swish
as I forced the foolish ball up
from anywhere on the court.
Who could explain it?
The ball had eyes, they said.
My fumble fingers grown
a logic all their own.

Until the last game
of the playoffs,
standing under the basket
all alone,
one free throw down
and five seconds to go,
shouting at the desperate guard,
the shot already
lifting from my fingers
as the ball came rolling
toward me, slow, too slow,
me, up there in the air
empty-handed, the ball slowly
rolling out the door
and down these many years,

rolling still,
careening off the fingertips
of every dumb mistake
I'd ever make.

And so, poised here, midair,
shouting for attention
to anyone who'll hear,
my hands above the rim,
I'm dreaming these words up
from nothing. Rebounding.
Stuffing them in.

Condoms

She says the book she is reading is gross.
She says she won't tell me what "gross" is.
Hours later, at bedtime, she asks about condoms.
I don't tell her
about the first rubber I ever saw,
fished out of a St. Louis drainage ditch in 1956,
dripping with sewage and ooze,
or about how Johnny Ferretti
blew them up like balloons
for the girls at the Country Day grade school,
or how "for the prevention of disease only"
we'd buy them in the men's room
of Bob Winston's Skelley Station
and keep them like IDs in our wallets.
Instead, I slip over them
that slick word, *prophylactics,*
and tell her they are a birth control device
used by two people making love.
When I bend down to kiss her
she pulls her head under the blankets.
Okay, she grimaces. *That's* gross.

Camp Calvary

Jack, the pastor's son, and only kid I know
at this damn camp, is off
necking with a counselor who's eighteen.
He's twelve. What does she see in him,
I wonder, as I trudge alone to archery
or crafts, to make a bull's-eye for
my mother, who sent me here
for God knows what perverted reason.
It's church camp. Every morning I pray
to be delivered from the squealing kids
who seem to be having such great fun
as I lie in wait inside my puny body
for time to pass and let me out.
What quirk of fate, what evil-minded
God has stuck me here? And does He sit
chuckling in His heaven, as water balloons
whizz by my ear, and my name takes shape
and sails out over the lunchroom
like a straw paper dipped in mashed potatoes
sticking to the ceiling for everyone to see?
Jack's a pock-marked, pimply kid, skinny
as a cigarette, smelling of smoke and mint.
He carries booze in a hip flask
and sells dirty pictures of his sister.
And what does it matter that his father
will one day be unfrocked, his mother
become the loony I always knew she was,
Vietnam, cocaine, and the Navy take him away
for keeps? Today he's gone off with the counselor,
and everybody loves him, and I am
climbing out of my midget's body, cursing,
and heading for the future
just as fast as the mind can see.

Smoking

I'm holding my cigarette out the car window,
hoping it will burn down faster
so I won't have to smoke it, the orange
tip sparking in the dark, turning to ash.

I'm fourteen, riding in the front seat
with a woman who should know better,
the pastor's son feeling her up
as her hands grip the wheel.

Oh grow up, they say, shoving
the Winstons at me with a match,
and I, too shy or stupid to protest,
do. We're riding through

this long night of adolescence,
Buddy Holly and the Big Bopper flopping
somewhere overhead, the future
stretched out filmy and seductive

on the bed of our separate thoughts:
the driver with our lives tight in her hands;
the pastor's son praying his way into her lacy bra;
my cigarette and my anger burning on

so long that thirty long years later,
after cancer and car accidents
have had their way with them,
they're still there, cruising along

the side streets of my memory,
lighting me up again and again
every time I try
to put them down.

Love and Sex

We did it in the car, in the dark
private girls' school parking lot
where we could watch the security guard
coming a long way off. Midwinter,
the old heater clattering, our underwear
wedged in the glove compartment, *hello
officer, yes, we were just leaving.*
How desire and longing could inspire
the unlikeliest situation, as we drove
home through the unconsummated snow,
all smiling, heat, and light.

How we work to get it perfect, now.
The queen size bed and fitted sheets,
the firelight glinting through the wine,
the familiar choreography of marital art,
the infinite variety we've got by heart.

Bible Stories

He served them after dinner
as our just deserts,
while I ate my canned
fruit cocktail, and scowled.
I was twelve, and longed to be
out in the steamy streets
with my multitude
of friends,
King of McKinley Avenue
if not the Jews.

Inside, my crippled father,
hunched over in his chair,
with barely strength to change
the flimsy pages
in that heavy book,
or air to wheeze
the morals of the Lord,
grimaced over stories
of Noah and his flood,
Aaron's fairy rod,
Sodom and Gomorrah,
the boring, innocent garden
he adored.

Inside, I was hopeless—
clumsy elbows on the table,
milk spilled on the floor,
broccoli languishing on my plate
so children in hungry India
could starve.

He was the mountain of commandments,
broken tablet, burning bush.
And I, no likely Moses,
a bogus magician, pillar of salt.

Outside, I drove swine
off the maddened cliffs,
waltzed across the shut-down
flooded quarry,
washed more than girls' insteps
with my hair,
multiplied my bullheads and my loaves.
Oh, I rose up
bright and shining, changing
water into wine,
and came home praised and prodigal
to my chastened, healed, forgiven
father's house.

Off the Record

In the attic I find the notes
he kept in college
over forty years ago: *Hooray*
for Thanksgiving vacation! he wrote
in the margin of Psych 102.
And for a moment I can see him there,

feel the exuberance surge through
that odd cell of his body
where I am still
a secret code uncompleted, a piece
of DNA, some ancient star-stuff.
And then I find a recording of me

from 1948, when he was twenty-two
and I was three, and I can see,
from my perch up on his shoulders,
him stopping at the gaudy arcade,
plugging his lucky quarter into
the future where we'd always be.

Maybe imagination is just
a form of memory after all, locked
deep in the double helix of eternity.
Or maybe the past is but one more
phantasmagoric invention we use
to fool ourselves into someone else's shoes.

It is not my voice I want to hear
on memory's fading page, on imagination's disk.
It is my father's in the background
prompting me, doing his best
to stay off the record, his hushed
instructions vanishing in static.

Fan Mail

When Marjorie, the information manager
of a chin-operated wheelchair company,
writes to say how much she liked my poem
about a *Mr. Wallace* who, paralyzed from
the neck down for twenty years, when
he got his first motorized wheelchair,
roared around the nursing home, carroming
off walls, tearing up linoleum, leaving
his mark on things again, making an
impression he hadn't made for years,
and finally crashed (figuratively, perhaps)
out the fourth floor picture window
of his recuperating room,
and sailed off in slow motion
trailing bright stars of glass,
and tells me she, too, has been paralyzed
from the neck down for so long she'd
thought her funny bone as well had gone,

I think about you again, father, slumped
in the vast doorway of the past, grinning
under the weight of a frame grown huge
on you, and how we sat those distant afternoons
in urine smell and silence, waiting
for the night nurse to lay you
one last time on that taut bed.
And so, when, in this chin-operated missive,
its five good-tempered sentences
tapped out with what intensive care, Marjorie
says if my *Mr. Wallace* is someone real I know
and love, and think could use her company,
then I should send her his address so
she can get in touch (there have been

such developments!), although it's been
ten years since you on this hard earth
have had a local habitation, I lift my chin.
I send this exultation in your name.

Speeding

Some damn fool kid
is racing his three-speed
down the hill in front of our house,
sailing off speed bumps,
splitting the road down the middle
as if it is his.
His new speedometer
clipped to his handlebars
reads 50 mph, he thinks,
but he can't be sure
because his eyes are tearing
in the wind
and it is all he can do
to keep from wiping out on the sand
left over from the late winter road crews.
The March sun is shining,
the wind kissing his face,
spring flashing its bright green signals,
although, approaching fast from a side street,
the future is looming,
preparing to barrel through.
Look out! I shout. But it's too late.
The kid has been gone for years,
pedaling for all he was worth
into me, into you.

II. Breakdown

Breakdown

When finally you know
you are not going to make it,
the car's heart failing
on this dark country road,
the night, which had so politely
stepped aside, crowding in on you
like a stranger in a bar
who wants more than you're
prepared to give him, or
the intruder you're sure
has entered your foyer at midnight
with his crowbar for your spine,

do you stop
at the broken-down farm house
looming like some monster of retribution,
old eggs and sweat in its breath,
swollen with children and hostility,
the smell pressing its great thumb
on your nostrils and eyelids,
the old man in his bloated undershirt
looking everywhere but at you,
his thick fist wriggling
in his greasy overalls, his wife
clutching her disgust tight
to her breast, the telephone hung
on the exposed lath, dead?

Or do you shake hands with that stranger,
let him buy you a drink, show him
your wallet and silver,
inhale his pomaded hair,
and cruise back to his place,

with its abandoned gas stations,
its policemen winking under streetlamps,
its pleasant houses where you know
it's too late to go?

Or will it matter when tomorrow—
that mechanic who's always shown up
so reliably before—comes back
with his bright lamp, his tools
and his expertise, and you drive home
to your own country, nothing changed,
except for this small uncertainty,
this fist in your gut, this sneer
twisting your lips, as if
you knew something true and awful,
something you could never, never confess.

Onions

The physicist, on my right, calls it
a culvert with wings, this sixteen-seater
prop plane that lopes its way from
Walla Walla, Yakima, and Pasco,
the Tri-City Area with its nuclear reactors,
its views of the Blue Mountains, its wheat,
its Walla Walla sweets. Last night
my wife was raped at rusty knife-point
on the streets of Walla Walla between
the Homestead Restaurant and the local 7-11.
Her assailant made off with her
car keys and shirt, leaving us diminished
to anger, and grief's slow heat.
The physicist is saying all that news
about fusion in a test tube is
so much hokum, it's a matter of
magnetic fields and donuts, of
containment—a hundred million degrees.
The plane hits an air pocket, a slight
disturbance, as we slide in our tenuous seats
over produce and plutonium at 17,000 feet.
It's simple physics, he assures us,
as we cling to our baggage of outrage,
the Blues, our Walla Walla sweets.

Hairpin

Suddenly, there is no road.
Your headlights glare into the darkness
looming up at you faster
than you can jackknife the wheel
or lay on the screaming brakes.
The green dash lights flash cockeyed
and you're rolling over and over
off the shoulder, through the culvert,
into the atrazined fields, the tiny
corn plants flattening out, making way.

And although you walk out of this,
miraculous, without even a scratch, unscathed,
your body keeps rolling and rolling,
your brain flashing its luminous messages
of speed, pressure, temperature, fuel
consumption, as, at even the quietest moments,
in the bright slow deceptions of day,
you race toward that sudden appointment
you'd never quite planned on,
that journey you didn't mean to take.

Headlines

When the car overturns and skids forty yards
on its roof, lurches over the curb and explodes,
and the neighbor, out getting the best of
the drought at two A.M., turns his pitiful garden hose
on the cinders for all he is worth, as if
something there could germinate, his words out of
control fluttering above him like moths
in the flickering helpless light: *I'm here!*
I'll save you! I'll save you all!
                                    do you
wake from a dreamless sleep to the reassuring
breathing of the bedrooms in your quiet house,
and then continue your long ride through the night
as though tomorrow's headlines can't affect you
after all, your own children under your wing,
safe inside the formal garden you've prepared
for them with all the care and artfulness you
could muster, morning careening just around the
corner, your own spring flagging, the drought burning on?

The Poetry Report

All across America poets
are working on the drought,
heads in the clouds tossing
their wordy seeds, out
in the fields with the metaphoric
corn, or tending their own
parched gardens. We've seen
it all before—the nearly empty
reservoirs, the dusty topsoil
blown half the way from Kansas
to New York, the sky
with its same blue message
day after day. The world
pays little attention,
accustomed as it is
to ease and plenty,
to subsidized overproduction.
If prices rise, and some small
voice goes under, it's probably
better in the long run. Oh,
the poets' brows are moist,
their thick tongues swollen
as they continue cultivating
a slow rain of language.
For them, the future, as always,
looks cloudy, as they go on
paring their worried fingernails
or muttering into their cups,
making nothing happen.

At Forty

Ladders sway away from houses
in the wind of the long way down.
Feet, even on level ground,
keep stubbing their toes on the concrete
as if trying to enter that country for which
their whole long life is the passport.
All winter, things go up in smoke.
The children grow lighter than air as though
no gravity's tug could hold them.
Who'd have thought death was so easy?
This slow fall on the wind,
this stroll past custom's lax border,
the way things let go
like a postscript from the past,
that last and best correspondent.

Turning Forty

Time doesn't speed up like a train
with somewhere to get to, railing
on that Augustinian straight line,

so much as it spirals, silent, circling
back on itself, an old dog, settling
on the same tired spot again

and again. So the new love, the thing,
the place you'd once have so longed
for, get lost in the past, are gone

almost before you've found them.
As memory, satisfied, fat, pushes
imagination aside, anticipation pales, and

events turn back to their own past selves,
no mental foreplay to warm them,
no heat left to expand or rise.

In the country of stumble and drag
time settles, its bald tail a-wag.

Professor of Plums

for Ricardo Quintana

Last week he might have been sleeping
through the lecture on Samuel Johnson
being given in his honor, had he not
opened his eyes occasionally
to laugh his walrus laugh,
his whole body shaking,
tossing some fruits and vegetables
toward the orator on the stage.

Crafty old fellow. Every Saturday morning
I'd see him in the supermarket
in the cottage cheese and eggs
or picking through the radishes and lettuce,
asking through his mustache could I
explicate an apple? Deconstruct a peach?
And then go wheeling cockeyed
down the aisle to beat the band,
whistling like a schoolboy
and nobody's grand old man.

And now I get this message
that his own heart has failed him,
has slumped like a student
too unprepared to speak.
Oh Professor of Plums, sweet
Tutor of Produce, may your soul
walrus its way up through
whatever long lectures
Dean Death may invent for you.
May you toss him some eggs and tomatoes.
May you chuckle through that long sleep.

State Poetry Day

The mayor couldn't be here, but he sends his grand whereases,
and his best regards take their places in the rear.
Another year closes with a villanelle's razzmatazzes.

Outside, in sunlight, with their stunted squash and radishes,
farmers wonder what the going rate is for crop failure and despair.
The mayor couldn't be here but he sends his grand whereases.

In the legislative chambers with their dactyls and caesuras
the local poet laureates sing in praise of cheese and beer.
Another year closes with a villanelle's razzmatazzes.

On the South Side, poverty makes another of its passes.
A bag lady lifts her breakfast from a trash can on the square.
The mayor couldn't be here but he sends his grand whereases.

Now the poetry club presidents show their poems off like badges
to the hard-of-hearing, blue-haired citizens gathered here.
Another year closes with a villanelle's razzmatazzes.

No one mentions Nicaragua, acid rain, cocaine, or Star Wars,
as the couplets and quatrains maintain a pleasant atmosphere.
The mayor couldn't be here, but he sends his grand whereases.
Another year closes with a villanelle's razzmatazzes.

The Dinner Party

Everyone out in the living room's concerned
about groundwater and nuclear war,
their voices a warm glow in the dark,
the familiar country of engaging party talk,
and I'm here in the kitchen with my spinach
and my eggs, my vinegar and oil, worrying

about how to make a salad. Worrying
is something I'm very good at. I've been concerned
over things much less important than spinach
which at this moment seems worse than war.
How much easier, I think, it is to talk
than actually do something. I'm in the dark

about this salad. Shall I add these dark
olives, these tomatoes? Should I be worrying
the oil into the vinegar? Do I talk
to the eggs and parsley, show my concern
to the celery? The ingredients are at war
as I wonder whether this is lettuce or spinach.

As a child I hated salads, hated spinach.
One night I was sent to my lonely dark
room for dawdling, not eating. A family war
erupted, my father shouting, my mother worrying
that I'd be damaged for life, her concern
radiating up through the floor. Their talk

filled the house with tear gas, talk
that tasted in my mouth worse than spinach.
I wished they had something else to be concerned
about, as I fled through the foreign dark
of their anger. They could have been worrying
about Hitler and the Second World War.

33

Out in the living room they've moved from war
to gourmet cooking in that easy way talk
has of absolving itself of all worry
in time. And now it's time for spinach.
Let groundwater keep its own dark
counsel, radiation be its own concern.

This is war. I serve up the goddamned spinach.
All talk ceases in the leafy dark.
On their lips: the oil of concern, the vinegar of worry.

The Hell Mural: Panel I

Iri and Toshi Maruki are "painting the bomb."
Their painting, they say, will comfort the souls of the dead.
"It's a dreadful cruel scene of great beauty,"
Toshi says. "The face may be deformed but there's kindness
in a finger or a breast, even in hell."
The Hell Mural spreads over the floor.

Iri stretches naked on the floor,
painting. He remembers Hiroshima after the bomb—
the bodies stacked up, arms outstretched toward hell,
nothing he could see that was not dead,
nothing that cared at all for human kindness,
nothing that wept at such terror, such beauty.

Now a brush stroke here, a thick wash there, and beauty
writhes and stretches from the canvas floor.
He wants his art to "collaborate with kindness,"
he wants his art to "uncover the bomb."
But no lifetime's enough to paint all the dead
or put all those who belong there in hell.

"Hitler and Truman," he says, "of course are in hell.
But even those of us who live for beauty
are in hell, no less so than the dead."
(He paints himself and Toshi on the floor.)
"All of us who cannot stop the bomb
are now in hell. It's no kindness

to say different. It's no kindness
to insist on heaven; there's only hell."
Toshi adds bees and maggots to the bomb,
and birds, cats, her pregnant niece, the beauty
of severed breast and torn limb on the killing floor.
"In Hiroshima," she says, "we crossed a river on the dead

bodies stacked up like a bridge. Now the dead
souls must be comforted with kindness.
Come, walk in your socks across our floor,
walk on the canvas. (A little dirt in hell
almost improves it.) Can you see the beauty
of this torso, that ear lobe, this hip bone of the bomb?"

Iri and Toshi Maruki, in "Hell," are painting the bomb,
the mural on their floor alive with the thriving dead.
Come walk on their kindness, walk on their troublesome beauty.

The Hell Mural: Panel II

Iri and Toshi Maruki are painting the bomb.
Their painting, they say, will comfort the souls of the dead
in Hiroshima, Nagasaki, Belsen, Dachau, and Vietnam.

Because Hitler and Truman and Nixon with such aplomb
could order the deaths of millions, then go to bed,
Iri and Toshi Maruki are painting the bomb.

They draw in bees and maggots, and then go on—
a nipple here, a finger there, a head—
to Hiroshima, Nagasaki, Belsen, Dachau, and Vietnam.

Birds, cats, naked men and women spawn
on the floor in their mural, burning—the beautiful dead
of Iri and Toshi Maruki's painting, the bomb.

They paint with kindness and beauty, as if that song
must be sung, that corpse embraced, those right words said:
Hiroshima, Nagasaki, Belsen, Dachau, and Vietnam.

All history's heroes are here to be walked upon,
and *we* are here, beneath their brushstrokes' tread.
In Iri and Toshi Maruki's painting, the bomb
is Hiroshima, Nagasaki, Belsen, Dachau, and Vietnam.

Fortunes

Although we have no illusions about
the efficacy of all this,
we let her look into our hands.
She's no professional, she says, but a damned
good amateur, which is no more or less
than anyone might reasonably expect.
Whether she knows all and sees all
is beside the point, if there is a point,
and we will assume there is.

She's not into futures, though she can tell
from the left hand what we've inherited,
and from the right how much
of that large legacy we've spent.
If we learn nothing more than that
we have a heart line, a life line,
a mount of Mars as good as the next man's,
and that we're passionate and imaginative enough
to have taken her husband's advice
and paid our fifty cents
to hold his good wife's hand,
why, haven't we gotten our money's worth?
Pleasure is good tender anywhere.

Or perhaps just the will
to believe in something is enough—
that our own pasts have marked us for better or worse
and that those small hairline fractures
we constantly palm off on the world
can give us guidance or pause.

Whatever the cause of our visitations,
we're all sending messages to each other daily,
our hands and words and eyes casting the light
that can go on for years, palms up,
searching for someone to read it.

We will purchase our small futures gladly
from whatever market will trade in them,
even this gypsy, the past,
that exchange that goes back
long before the flat hand of this earth
clenched up its round fist,
long before the stars, even, began
sending their friendly messages,
which we get only now,
that they are there. Or were there, once.

III. *The Makings of Happiness*

Building an Outhouse

Is not unlike building a poem: the pure
mathematics of shape; the music of hammer
and tenpenny nail, of floor joist, stud wall,
and sill; the cut wood's sweet smell.

If the Skil saw rear up in your unpracticed hand,
cussing, hawking its chaw of dust,
and you're lost in the pounding particulars
of fly rafters, siding, hypotenuse, and load,
until nothing seems level or true
but the scorn of the tape's clucked tongue,

let the nub of your plainspoken pencil prevail
and it's up! Functional. Tight as a sonnet.
It will last forever (or at least for awhile)
though the critics come sit on it, and sit on it.

Wiffle Ball

Doing my best to hit
the bat, I serve the pitch up
on a platter.
Limp-wristed and slithery
she spins full around
and falls to the ground
dizzy, a fizzle.
Despair floats out
to the makeshift mound
and I catch it.
So I explain
stance, the snap
of the wrist, the quick
eye and level swing, the love
of the game—
all curve balls
to her blunt stare.
And what do I care
anyway? She's nine, and I
can't make her do
anything she doesn't
want to, so there!
She stumps off adjusting
her mask and pads,
shaking off all my signs.

Basketball

The ball, almost
as big as she is,
hefted above her head,
she looks up into
the bright orange rim
of the sun. She's six
and the backboard sky
might just as well be
93 million miles away.
Stubs of burdock erupt
all around us
on our court of dirt and hay.
Hurry up, I shout.
We don't have all day.
And we don't.
The next time I look
she's sixteen, the years
arcing up and falling
with a curt swish,
her laughter spinning off
her fingertips, as
the future, all elbows and hips,
sets its practiced pick.

Barn Swallows

All morning they've flittered,
erratic, to the pond,
pinching mud in their beaks, then straw,
to daub under the porch eaves.
The nest grows, cosy as a woven bonnet.

I wonder why they chose
to build here right over my head,
while the whole barn they're named for
goes begging? They dive bomb me once
with every small load,
the thin air turned palpable, dangerous.

With one thrust of my putty knife
I could undo the day's work
and send these mad hatters packing.
Instead, I move off to a safe distance
and watch them stitch the air,
looping the thread of their flight
against me, pulling it tight.

Frogs

The fact that the cat
just ate the frog
that had been singing all night
of its lovemaking,
trilling its rickety chords,
its whirs and chitters and clicks,
riding the back of its beloved
in the luxury of our two-bit pond,
somehow, more than is reasonable
or right, troubles you

in our bed this Sunday morning,
light streaming in through
the unwashed windows
past the wilting sheets
into the dilating black hole
of your eye, for which, I think,
what frog, riding the current
of its short life
into the end of everything
it will ever know
or care to know,
wouldn't die?

Fall

The goats are out again,
over the inner gate
and out the window of the shed.
You can't keep them in
any more than you can
joy or rage.
Five A.M. in our sunny bed
we hear them, clattering
on the pump platform,
reaching for the leaves
of every small tree we've planted.
A mouthful or two and
there's nothing left, just
stiff twigs pointing out the sky.
September. Last month
I would have dragged them back, kicking,
to their bedstraw pen.
This morning I
leave them to their pleasures
as we climb out of
ourselves and into a country
of such flowers and trees
who'd believe some cold hand
could drag us back to
ourselves again, could
bring us to our knees?

Poet in the Goat Yard

What am I doing
out here in the goat yard,
the red sun setting on the pasture,
this syringe in my hand full of Tylan
("for cattle and swine only,
has been fatal in equine uses"),
wondering whether a goat is more
like a cow or a pig or a horse?
I, who am so lavish with analogies,
who can so carelessly crossbreed
sun and blood or death and levity
or kids and kids, find myself
blind in the sweet eye of this alpine,
bleating for help. My daughter
clings to my shirt sleeves for assurance
as I lift the bright syringe,
a needle of health, I tell her,
a splinter of sun, thinking:
That language were so powerful, so dangerous!
Goat, I sing, *be pig, be*
cow: root and snort and wallow
from your snout to your curly tail;
bellow and ruminate and moo
down the length of your leathery hide;
make me good as my word.
I raise my dangerous hand
and it's done. The sun sets on
the goat yard, this she goat, and my daughter.
Who's to say song doesn't matter?
She falls to her small knees, bleating
her one song after another.

Roosters

Locked in the milk house,
cut off from the rest of the flock
to keep their crops empty,
the roosters flutter and squawk.

Cock crow at noon,
at two, and four o'clock.
The fat hens, abandoned
in the shade of the August burdock,

warble and croon
in what might suffice for sadness,
until you stick your neck out
and joke: *poultrygeists*, and we laugh

through the long afternoon
as we lop, pluck, gut, crow, and yodel,
the sky boiling up around us,
the red sun flashing like a hatchet.

The Fox in the Berry Patch

Walking the goats through the oak woods,
pausing to browse on the tangle
of raspberries and prickly ash,
we come across a fox. It
seems smaller than its reputation—
chicken-stealer, crow bait, outlaw,
sly quarry of hound and horn.
Still, there is an exhilaration
in the fox itself,
or in the first-time seeing.
We stop breathing.
The goats go on eating.

Earlier, we talked about meaning.
How ease inhabits our lives.
How these leisurely acres in the country
debunk all hunger and need.
It is America's dilemma, we conceded,
and went on gardening.

Now, high on this razorback ridge
this small fox confronts us
without care, or fear, or heat.
Is he hungry? Does he want something
from us? He sidles closer as if
indifferent to our size and means.
For one moment I imagine
having to throw the goats at him,
or kicking with my swift feet.
But then he returns to his brambles.
And we return to our berry patch
and eat and eat and eat.

Apple Cider

Breezy with bees
apple pulp rises under the grinder,
shreds of flesh and skin glistening,
the amber liquid dripping
into the tin acidic bucket.

September. Last month
your grandmother was murdered
by some incidental drifter
who cracked her in his arms
until her poor heart burst.

It is as if every death
is the first death: My father
red with bedsores; our daughter
swollen bright beyond us.
Can God want such a harvest?

Memory squeezes us dry
beyond sweetness, beyond weeping,
our twisted expressions turning
pulp into the compost
for the long winter ahead.

We lift our cup of sorrows,
burn our taciturn tongues,
and then this wild embracing, as
the bees go on about their business
making threats and honey.

Astronomy

Armed with my luminous star map,
I leave the bright house behind—
the whir and chitter of the refrigerator,
the tick of the pendulum clock,
the faint breathing of miniature sleepers,
and walk into the charted dark. There are
so many more stars in the country,
nothing to swallow them up.

At dusk we came across
a fox in the middle of the trail, sleeping.
We called its name, barked to startle it.
But it lay there, motionless, indifferent.
Sick, perhaps. Or wounded. We thought
probably hunters or dogs. You
wanted to take it home, save it.
When we came back later, it was gone.

My star map imparts a fierce clarity—
The Big Dipper, Cassiopeia, Pegasus,
Cygnus, Draco, and this milky blur
of a galaxy moving off from us
in its motionlessness and indifference,
though we go on saving, naming it,
as if the sleeping constellations, even,
needed our help.

Night in the Country

The sky shimmers and cracks, a crystal glass.
Great wavy rifts drift through the valley of stars.
At first we think our eyes are playing tricks
on us, some ocular jest shifting the atmosphere
mercilessly. We laugh perhaps at the end of
the world, its last joke these flaccid bones of sky.
Far from the city with its bright deceptions,
we lie down in the damp grass and await whatever
blast of heat or radiance is on its way to take us
out of ourselves into the future that couldn't be.
Tomorrow, the papers will claim aurora borealis,
a rare display for those with dark enough to see.
But tonight, together on this rural lawn,
we wonder what lovely, terrible script is written
across the galaxy, the stars clustered above us
like stars, or the memory of stars.

February, Full Moon

Two A.M. The full moon ringed with haze.
I'm out behind the farm house,
alone in the uncharitable dark,
the crusted snow, bright as mica,
lightening under my weight
in this mid-February silence.

Inside, the warm house brightens
as if the click of the refrigerator
and the slow breathing of the children
could call up the whippoorwill,
cicada, spring peeper, and cricket,
could fill us beyond loss or doubt,

as the hills step off into whiteness,
into bony, emaciated want.
Famished and ravenous season,
what privilege calls you lovely?
Snow moon, wolf moon, hunger moon,
what heartlessness calls you full?

February Thaw

Flickers at the feeder;
a puff of nuthatch on the beech;
the roadside mud quick with rivulets;
a sputter of crocus and jonquil;
two red-tails aflame.

Lord, how our charred eyes brighten!

Tonight, mindful of its livelihood,
winter will go about its business
dowsing these unlikely fires,
the tin stars pinned
in the tenpenny wind.

Prayer

Could it be so simple as the low
sun making of the old farmstead
one great rose window?

Or the votive candles of snow
over which one crow,
cowled in its own shadow, lengthens?

All day the day has been darkening,
the long night coming on.
And then this acolyte sun

setting the landscape aglow,
the wick of your own breath aflutter:
rose window, candle, crow.

Burning

Sunset. The front yard catches fire;
sparks start from the blackened grass,
rise in the stammering air:
So many fireflies, or stars!

Dear, the old world is burning;
tomorrow the new world will flare.
We'll awake to the conflagration:
boneset, bee balm, love grass, blazingstar.

In the Amish Bakery

I don't know why what comes to mind
when I imagine my wife and daughters,
off on a separate vacation
in the family car,
crashing—no survivors—
in one of those Godless snowstorms
of Northern Illinois,
is that Amish bakery
in Sauk County, Wisconsin, where,
on Saturday mornings in summer,
we used to go—
all powdered sugar and honey in
the glazed caramel air. And O
the browned loaves rising,
the donuts, buns, and pies, the ripe
strawberry stain of an oven burn
on the cheek of one of the wives.
And outside in the yard
that goddamned trampoline
where we'd imagine them—
the whole blessed family in
their black topcoats and frocks,
their severe hair and beards,
their foolish half-baked grins,
so much flour dust and leaven—
leaping all together on
their stiff sweet legs toward heaven.

The Fat of the Land

Gathered in the heavy heat of Indiana,
summer and 102°, we've come from
all over this great country,
one big happy family, back from
wherever we've spread ourselves too thin.
A cornucopia of cousins and uncles, grand-
parents and aunts, nieces and nephews, expanding.
All day we laze on the oily beach;
we eat all the smoke-filled evening:
shrimp dip and crackers,
Velveeta cheese and beer,
handfuls of junk food, vanishing.
We sit at card tables, examining
our pudgy hands, piling in
hot fudge and double chocolate
brownies, strawberry shortcake and cream,
as the lard-ball children
sluice from room to room.
O the loveliness of so much loved flesh,
the litany of split seams and puffed sleeves,
sack dresses and Sansabelt slacks,
dimpled knees and knuckles, the jiggle
of triple chins. O the gladness
that only a family understands,
our fat smiles dancing
as we play our cards right.
Our jovial conversation blooms and booms
in love's large company, as our sweet
words ripen and split their skins:
mulberry, fabulous, flotation,
phlegmatic, plumbaginous.
Let our large hearts attack us,
our blood run us off the scale.

We're huge and whole on this simmering night,
battened against the small skinny
futures that must befall all of us,
the gray thin days and the noncaloric dark.

The Makings of Happiness

"If a man can't be happy on a little farm in Wisconsin,
he hasn't the makings of happiness in his soul."

Until you have looked at something so long
it grows so familiar you can't see it—
the alp that all but disappears in dailiness;
the sea that common routine conceals;
the little farm in Wisconsin that seems
painted in oil on your long picture window,
its thick cow turned toward you, wryly
rolling its eyes, stymied by all this hoopla,
its stiff farmer, pinned to his blue ribbon,
pressed in his Sunday best, levitating,
its grinning photographer, tipping
what could be a black beret,
as if this were Marseilles or Paris
and not Hollandale, Wisconsin, 1922,
the war to end all wars now over,
the barn more like a hearth than a barn,
a mother, who could be your mother,
in the doorframe across the way,
bread in the oven and time on her hands,
the little girl, who could be a boy,
roped to her calf, which could be a dog,
waving to her cat, which could be a stoat,
apples in her cheeks and honey in her hair,
the church in the permanent center,
the townspeople happy as larks,
the scene flat and perspectiveless,
a child's colorful cutout—
you'll not know the soul's work:
to keep the man floating, the girl

smiling, the calf changing, the cow rolling
its eyes, the blue Frenchman tipping
his hat at you who live so far off
in the vanishing point of the future.

About the Author

RONALD WALLACE was born in 1945 in Cedar Rapids, Iowa, and grew up in St. Louis, Missouri. He was educated at the College of Wooster (Ohio) and the University of Michigan. He is Director of Creative Writing at the University of Wisconsin in Madison, and series editor of the Brittingham Prize in Poetry of the University of Wisconsin Press. He divides his time between Madison and a forty acre farm in Richland County, Wisconsin.

Pitt Poetry Series

Ed Ochester, General Editor